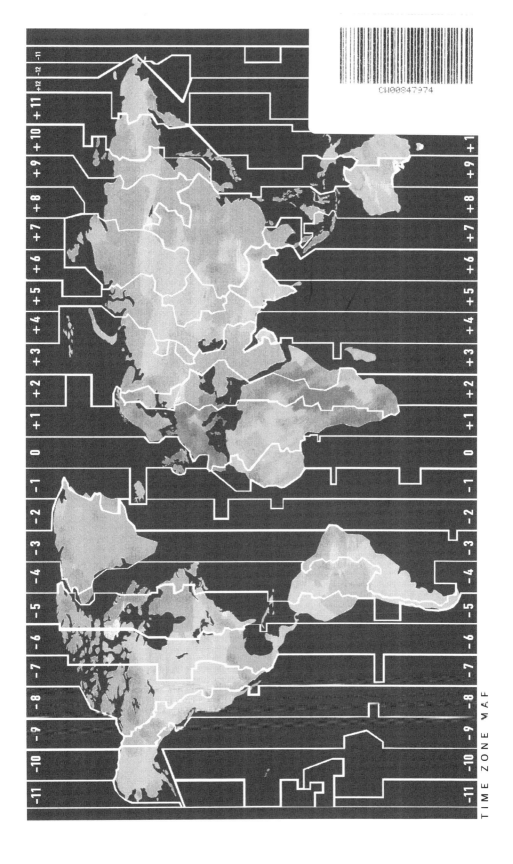

CW00847974

TIME ZONE MAP

DESTINATION(S):

GOOD TO KNOW ABOUT REGION AND CULTURE:

Don't go to Central park at Night

Holiday Shops

Bryant park
opens 11:00 - 20.00hs
situated behind NY public Library
in midtown, Manhattan
between 40th & 42nd street
Take B, D, F or M train to 42nd St.
Also situated by 5th & 6th Avenue
Take the 7 train to 5th Avenue

PACKING LIST

- [ ] Doc Martens
- [ ] Thick Socks
- [ ] Thermal Vests

- [ ] Print Insurance Docs
- [ ]
- [ ]
- [ ]
- [ ]
- [ ]
- [ ]
- [ ]
- [ ]
- [ ]
- [ ]
- [ ]
- [ ]
- [ ]
- [ ]
- [ ]
- [ ]
- [ ]
- [ ]
- [ ]
- [ ]
- [ ]
- [ ]
- [ ]
- [ ]
- [ ]
- [ ]
- [ ]
- [ ]
- [ ]
- [ ]
- [ ]
- [ ]
- [ ]
- [ ]
- [ ]
- [ ]

BUCKET LIST

- [ ] Empire State Building
- [ ] Macy's
- [ ] Breakfast at Tiffany's
- [ ] Bloomingdale
- [ ] Statue of Liberty
- [ ] 911 Museum
- [ ] Central Park
- [ ] Horse & Carriage Ride
- [ ] Broadway Show
- [ ]
- [ ]
- [ ]
- [ ]
- [ ]
- [ ]
- [ ]
- [ ]
- [ ]
- [ ]
- [ ]
- [ ]
- [ ]
- [ ]
- [ ]
- [ ]
- [ ]
- [ ]
- [ ]
- [ ]
- [ ]

BUDGET

TOTAL:	TOTAL:

BA MAN - LHR   1389
Departs 09.50
Arrives LHR   11.05

LHR - JFK - world Traveller plus
BA Flight 115
Departs LHR at 14.00
Arrives JFK at 17.10

Arlo Midtown Hotel

LOCATION:
NYC

DATE: WED
21 DEC

Embarkment Day - Queen Mary

- Smart Attire

Gala Evening - Black & white

Christmas Eve
- Smart Attire

Gala Evening - Red & Gold

- Smart Attire
- Take a ferry to St. John Island
  (approx $9) or get a taxi
  at the port.

SMART ATTIRE

- Discover Nevis Island
   Moira & Fiona

- Golf at Royal St. Kitts
   Nigel & Micky

Smart Attire

- Smart Attire

Visit Maho Beach
Get taxi from cruise terminal,
or pre book with Victor
approx £38 each for half day.
- Link with Marigot open air
  markets, coffee shops, French
  pastries.
- Also look at Mullet Bay,
  Orient Bay Beach or
  Philipsburg to fulfil the day.

GALA EVENING

SMART ATTIRE

SMART ATTIRE

BA Flight 114
Depart 21.45 (9.45 PM)
Group transfer to airport

DESTINATION(S):

GOOD TO KNOW ABOUT REGION AND CULTURE:

PACKING LIST

BUCKET LIST

BUDGET

| TOTAL: | TOTAL: |

LOCATION: DATE:

LOCATION: DATE:

LOCATION: DATE:

LOCATION: DATE: